DO TEAM

HOW TO GET THE BEST FROM EVERYONE

CHARLIE GLADSTONE

For my A team: Caroline, Jack, India, Tara, Xanthe, Kinvara, Felix, Reyhan, Dave and Aphra

Published by
The Do Book Company 2021
Works in Progress Publishing Ltd
thedobook.co

Text © Charles Gladstone 2021
Illustrations © Matt Blease 2021

To find out more about our company, books and authors, please visit **thedobook.co** or follow us **@dobookco**

5 per cent of our proceeds from the sale of this book is given to The Do Lectures to help it achieve its aim of making positive change: **thedolectures.com**

Cover designed by James Victore
Book designed and set by Ratiotype

Printed and bound by OZGraf Print on Munken, an FSC-certified paper

MIX
Paper from responsible sources
FSC® C163799

A CIP catalogue record for this book is available from the British Library

ISBN 978-1-907974-88-5

10 9 8 7 6 5 4 3 2 1

CONTENTS

INTRODUCTION

This book is about people. It's about working together towards a common goal — day in, day out. It's about making that shared experience a positive one. People are everything. In business, at home, on the street, the way that you treat people will alter the course of your life, and theirs. It's a wonderful, beneficent power that we all have; it's your gift. This book is a guide on how to develop your skills to use this power to get the best from everyone.

Unless you're a hermit, you need to be part of a team. Come to think of it, even hermits need teams at some point: maybe to help them build their hermit house, but definitely when they get sick and need to go to hospital.

But it's not just a matter of *need*. Good teams make life happier, more productive, more efficient and more fun. Being a part of a functioning team, wherever you sit in its hierarchy, is truly special. It requires focus, attention to detail and regular adjustment, but the rewards — both individually and collectively — are huge.

This book will show you how to get along with everyone you encounter and get the best from them. And, in so doing, build the best team you can.

If you're thinking, 'I pretty much work by myself, I don't need a team,' you're wrong. A team can be two people, or it can be a thousand. You form a team with your accountant and bank manager, with the people you hang out with or play sport with. A team just needs the right human energy at its core. It isn't an inanimate thing; it's a living, breathing organism.

Oh, and one other thing before we start. The biggest mistake I made in business — and it took me years to figure this out — was to try to do everything by myself. Things are different now, so I write from experience.

BE MORE ARCADE FIRE

How do you define a team? Well, let me put it like this. Imagine a full symphony orchestra of around a hundred people playing in full flow, all synchronised perfectly, deep in the music, focusing on the conductor and their instrument and nothing else, happy, consumed, well drilled, playing beautifully. That's a team. Or imagine football players on a pitch moving together with such poise and confidence that they take your breath away. At Anfield Stadium, when the Liverpool FC players are working together at their imperious best, the fans sing, 'Poetry in motion', and they have a point. Manager Jürgen Klopp's players know precisely what is expected of them and how to deliver. That's a team.

Back in 2012, my wife Caroline and I took our three older children to see the band Arcade Fire in Paris. We have seen them many times but there was one moment that night when this hyper-creative, multi-instrumentalist gang of friends hit their stride so beautifully (during 'Keep the Car Running', in case you're wondering) that there was true magic in the air. Feet on the monitors, deep in flow, hearts beating as one. I worked in music for many years and I have seen thousands of bands, but that was one of the few moments of pure alchemy that I've ever witnessed. And why did it work so well? Yup, you guessed it, because they came together as a team.

Your life may seem more prosaic than that of professional musicians or footballers, but once you've read this book you'll understand that, with the right focus and techniques, you can run a team that is every bit as beautiful and in sync.

MY FIRST TEAM

Over the last 33 years, I've started a number of new businesses and I now employ around 120 people, maybe a few more. There have been some amazing times, and some truly awful ones. I don't think that I'm a particularly good businessman. I'm quite good at ideas and thinking on my feet, and I have lots of energy, but I'm not that good at making lots of money — which is, of course, the standard criterion by which we judge business success.

But what I am good at is people. I like people. I'm interested in them. And as a result of that, I seem to be good at creating engaged, happy and productive teams that drive our businesses forward through passion, commitment, hard work and fun. Many people who work with me have stuck around for a long time, some for over twenty years.

Along the way, probably through necessity, I decided to redefine my notion of success. I used to believe that business success was purely financial. Not any more. Of course, your business needs to make a profit. But it doesn't need to make you rich. Today I don't care about that because I view success as something deeper, more personally enriching. I see it as happiness for me and for those that I work with.

Although this definition lies at the heart of this book, it's important to say that financial success and team success are intimately entwined. From good teams working collaboratively flow profit *and* happiness.

Being good with people and building happy teams are critical to the future of any business, whether large or small. Our world is changing: money alone is not enough; quality of life is vital. If our generation didn't know this before the Covid lockdowns of 2020 and 2021 then we do now. True empathy, kindness and generosity of spirit towards our fellow human beings cannot be the work of computers. People matter more than ever.

A lot of the management skills that I talk about in the book are often described as involving emotional intelligence, which is a relatively contemporary term. I'm glad that it's become a *thing* because I believe it to be far more valuable and interesting than conventional intelligence. The good news is that—unless you're a sociopath (good luck with that)—you can *learn* emotional intelligence. Some people learn it from an early age and that's a blessing. But don't worry if you struggle with certain aspects—I'm here to help.

Lastly, I should add that I don't believe I am that much better at anything than anyone else. So, this book will try not to be preachy. I am not saying I am absolutely right, and my way is the only way. But these methods *are* effective. They have worked for me and my teams over the last twenty or so years.

Do Team is a chronicle of my experience and how I've managed to get the best from those I live with, work with, even those that I fleetingly encounter. It's not hypothesis. It's a simple, effective, practical guide to building a team, whether at work or at home, for a weekend or a lifetime.

OK, let's get started.

EMOTIONAL INTELLIGENCE

CHAPTER 1
THE PRE-TEAM

When I was at school, and later at university, I loved building teams. I wasn't great at sport, so I'm not talking about anything competitive; mostly I brought people together to make plays, start a band and throw parties. Early on, I saw that when people work well together, they can be truly effective. We were chaotic, confused and hormonal but we did some good things because we had a common goal in sight. Those creative teams were one of the highlights of my education.

Soon after I left university, I got married. Caroline and I were 23 and had met just 16 months earlier. We didn't overthink it. We just did it. Over thirty wonderful years later, this team of two has raised six children, started a festival, opened shops, cafés and holiday cottages, run a pub, co-authored a book, renovated several derelict homes, tried (and often failed) to train endless dogs, and so much more. It hasn't always been easy, far from it. It hasn't always been fun, though there's been a great deal of that, but it has taught us about working together and the power of even the smallest of teams.

A good team isn't a luxury if you want to get stuff done; it's a necessity.

My first career was in the music industry. I was a self-employed music publisher and the manager of a mildly successful pop group. I spent much of this time living in a bubble. I employed a few people but I didn't really engage with them, certainly not emotionally. At the time, I thought that I had to shield everyone from any worries or concerns to do with the business, to put on a brave face, to figure out problems by myself. I would just ruminate until I came up with a solution.

After a few years it all came crashing down. I was working brutally hard, travelling a lot, stressed and exhausted, and the business had major cashflow issues. And, inevitably, I was often failing as a father and husband. Everything became too much and the business started to collapse.

What I learned was that I should have had a partner, even a mentor, from the beginning. I had a lovely, very approachable lawyer, but I didn't share any problems with him. With the benefit of hindsight, I know he would have been an excellent mentor or business adviser, and I am pretty sure he would have enjoyed acting as one — if only I'd asked him. But, most importantly, I eventually realised that I had a great team working for me but that I didn't work *with* them.

Over the coming years, as I worked on other businesses, I began to change my behaviour. I became more open and honest. I called on others to actually help me with problems and strategy. Piece by piece, we started to build a proper team and, from there, things started to function much better. Today I'd go so far as to say we're thriving.

FIRST STEPS

Employing others is a big step. Having staff on payroll is one of your biggest overheads so it's not something to rush into. But there are plenty of ways in which you can build an initial team without having the added stress of paying monthly salaries in the early stages of running a business when cashflow can be unpredictable.Some choose to work with a business partner, sharing investment and equity. Two clever, engaged, hard-working people are often more likely to make a success of a new business than one.

If you don't have someone who would make a suitable business partner, or you'd prefer to develop things yourself for the time being, then do consider having a mentor or some other form of business adviser. Experienced people are often happy to help. These days, I help a lot of people, even if it's just a chat on the phone to talk through an idea. I generally explain that what I have to offer is not a panacea but that I might have something useful to contribute.

The best way to find a mentor is to ask around. See if your parents, friends or friends' parents might know someone who works in a similar industry, or simply has the benefit of accumulated work experience. Then contact them. Don't be shy. Just send them an email introducing yourself and explaining what you're up to and that you would be grateful for any help or insight they might be able to offer. Of course, not everyone will be able or willing to help you, but you'll be surprised by how many people are more than happy to do so. If at first you don't succeed, try someone else.

When you find someone, listen to them and don't demand too much. Prepare for your sessions well and extract the maximum you can from them. I help a few

people in this way and I think they find it useful, but —
and this is important to remember — *I* find it enjoyable,
rewarding and educational. So, like many of the good
things in life, it's win win.

And remember that you probably already have people
around you who could be viewed as an early-stage team.
People who are working in the wider industry, such as
manufacturers, lawyers, accountants, even the nice people
in the tax office. Ask them questions. Share your concerns.
Don't pretend that everything is hunky-dory when it might
not be or things are beyond your comprehension. If you
treat them with respect, generosity and honesty, they will
repay you with the same.

ONE DAY YOU'LL NEED TO HIRE SOMEONE

If you've worked effectively with your (unofficial) team of
mentors and advisers then, one day, when you've started
trading and have some money in the bank, and more work
than you can cope with, you'll need to employ someone.
This is when it gets interesting and you truly need to figure
out how to build a proper team and get the best from people.

CHAPTER 2
GETTING THE FOUNDATIONS RIGHT

Have you ever seen *The Apprentice* with its pantomime baddies Sugar and Trump? In general, business isn't like that, and it certainly doesn't *need* to be. *The Apprentice* is entertainment. Depressing and rather vacuous entertainment, but it's entertainment, nonetheless.

No worthwhile business is just about the money. It's about people, joy, respect, kindness, fun, tolerance and the oxygen of praise and friendship. In fact, there's no reason why business shouldn't be like life outside the office when it's lived well; there's no reason why the two should differ.

At the root of all this are kindness and respect. Treat everyone that you encounter as you would like to be treated yourself. Kindness is strength and it's contagious. Be kind *for yourself*, because it is who you are. Don't do it for others, because it will impact on them anyway. Kindness spreads like a beautiful virus. This is not a hippy manifesto. It's a serious way of looking at the world and how it works. And it is foundational to your business and your team building.

HUMAN PURPOSE

Before you start to build your team, you need to define your *human purpose*. This is a key part of what is commonly referred to as company culture. In other words, how the people within your organisation interact with one another and with your customers; your company values, that sort of thing. The way your team operates will be defined by this so it's important to give it some thought before you start hiring. In order to define this human purpose, ask yourself the following questions. This is an important list, so take your time — you may even want to jot down your answers, if not now then later. We'll be covering many of these areas in the chapters that follow. Either way, your responses could well inform everything you do.

■ How do I define success? Is it just about money or something deeper?

■ What is the human purpose of my company? Do I want to value *people* as much as money?

■ Do I truly believe in the importance and power of people?

■ What human qualities am I looking for? What sort of people do I want to hire?

■ How important is trust to me? How do I learn to trust the people I work with? How do I get them to trust me?

■ How do I encourage and nurture the very best ideas?

■ How do I intend to lead by example?

- How am I going to deal with conflict without deviating from core values such as kindness and compassion?

- How do I make people comfortable with change?

- What will our company culture be when it comes to interacting with the outside world? How do we reply to emails? Do we value punctuality, good manners, relationships with suppliers?

- How will we behave in tough times? (There will be plenty of these, so it's something to think about before starting out.)

- How do I build and nurture real respect for all of those that we work with, both in our team and outside it?

- If I'm going to work with friends, family or partners, what rules will we put in place for behaviour at work?

- What sort of behaviour is unacceptable?

- How do I intend to go 'above and beyond' to care for those that I employ?

Don't worry if you don't have all of the answers right now. You will do once you've read this book.

COMPANY PURPOSE

You also need to be clear about your *company purpose*. In other words, why you're doing what you're doing and how you're going about it. This helps you, your team and your customers understand what you're about and what you're trying to change. My friend David Hieatt is the master here and his book *Do Purpose*, from the same publisher, is the perfect guide. So, add that to your bookshelf if you haven't already.

What interests me are the things that your customers might not necessarily see, but which they can *feel* when they interact with you. The real magic happens when these intentions have the support and drive of great people working together to make it happen. You can have the best idea in the world but if you don't work effectively with other people, each and every day, then your idea probably won't work, or if it does, may not endure.

You might make the best leather belts in the world or give the best haircuts or accountancy advice. You know exactly why you're doing it and are able to articulate that. Maybe you have a beautifully designed workplace and free coffee, even a ping-pong table in reception, but that's all pointless if you don't have a happy, productive, honest, trustworthy team that hang around and grow with you.

Money is not enough. Friendship, common goals, respect for your colleagues, kindness, compassion and so on are vital for this to work. It's time to find some people.

It takes strength to be gentle and kind.

The Smiths, 'I Know It's Over'

CHAPTER 3
CHOOSING THE RIGHT PEOPLE

You've launched your company and things are ticking over to the point that you're starting to feel over-stretched. It's time to think about employing someone, even if just for a couple of days a week. Moreover, you've defined your human purpose and have decided that building a great team is going to be critical to your success in both the short and long term. All you need to do now is find someone to work with you.

STICK THE TROMBONIST BEHIND A CURTAIN

There is a habit that needs to be avoided when hiring and it's this: we tend to gravitate towards people that we like the look of in the same way that we choose who to talk to at a party full of strangers. It's natural to select people who look or feel familiar to you. But sometimes I go to a large creative agency and everyone seems to look more or less the same. I can't help thinking, are these really the best people or do they just *look* like the best people?

I've heard stories about orchestras auditioning people by making them play behind a curtain. This might suggest that orchestras are trying to redress a gender or diversity imbalance, for example, or that it is simply better to select a musician blind because, that way, all you have to judge is the sound they make. But either way there is a lesson here: try to leave your personal preferences and any prejudices out of the hiring process. Physical impressions are important, but they are not everything. Diversity and variety will *always* bring fresh and original approaches to your company.

First things first, the job description. Make sure that you are as clear as you can be about the role on offer. Be precise about what it is that you need the successful candidate to do if they join you. This sounds elementary, I know. At a small company the job description is usually more open than at a big company because the person you employ is probably going to have to do a million different things. But try to be really clear what the candidate's key tasks or responsibilities will be.

Acknowledge every applicant. It's amazing how arrogant many companies can be. It isn't difficult to say, 'Thank you for applying. We'll be in touch if we need anything else from you.' Put yourself in the applicant's shoes.

You must give yourself time to read every CV and application letter. If you can, ask someone to work alongside you on the whole process, from start to finish. Ideally this would be someone who knows your business and whose opinion you value (a mentor or adviser, for example). Try and go through the applicants' CVs individually and then together.

Once you have a few suitable applicants, I would recommend sending them easy-to-digest notes about your company and what the job involves before they come to the interview. Tell them something about what you do, how you do it and what you want them to do. This will help 'sell' your company but more importantly, it will save time when you meet and, simultaneously, allow you to ask searching questions which may well reveal how interested the candidate actually is in the job.

You will then need to do some preparation ahead of the interview. Draw up some sheets with questions and a simple but really clear scoring system for each question (where 1 is wrong for the job and 5 is perfect). You need to ask everyone the same questions. Keep the questions open. 'Yes' or 'No' answers aren't of much use. You want to encourage each candidate to do the talking. Remember the interview is about them, not you, so try to avoid talking about yourself and the company. Save this for 'Any questions?' at the end.

When scheduling interviews, remember that the process is going to be tiring for you and that a tired interviewer is an ineffective one. Don't try to do too much in one day. Depending on the number of applicants you have, I'd say that eight half-hour sessions are more than enough. And remember to leave time between sessions.

OK, so now you will need to meet and interview your candidates. You have your questions ready and maybe even someone else sitting alongside you. Here are my recommendations for a successful interview process. Remember it's important — this person could well be your first member of the team!

- **Start on time.**

- **Be courteous and welcoming.** Know their name. Put the interviewee at ease as quickly as you can. Offer them a drink.

- **Don't be a 'people-pleaser'; keep it professional.** If they like you, they like you. If they don't, tough.

- Ask, listen, make notes, score.

- **Don't employ someone if their main concern seems to be the salary.**

- In particular, **ask them what they think of your company.** They need to feel the passion.

- **Never employ someone who is disrespectful about a current or former employer.**

After the interview, run through the candidates as thoroughly as you can with your associate. But don't make your mind up immediately. Give yourself at least a day to let everything settle. And don't forget to trust your gut feeling. Do you actually like the person? This is more important than you think.

Once you have decided on someone, always contact referees to double-check on them. Do this once you are pretty sure that this person is the one for you, and tell them that you're going to do so. Some people do this once the job has been offered and accepted.

Don't worry if your chosen candidate says 'no' to the job offer. It was not meant to be. And don't change the terms to please someone unless you are certain you are doing the right thing. Lastly, you may need to be flexible on salary if you can. It's worth paying a bit more to get the right person.

Always let unsuccessful candidates know that they won't be joining you. It's a basic courtesy.

And maybe you don't have to hire the most fully formed, experienced person in the world. Maybe it's what you do together when they join you that counts, how well you function as a team. So, follow your gut.

Lastly, hiring the wrong person is stressful and time-consuming. Not least, telling someone that they no longer have a job is a lot harder than offering them that job in the first place, so take your time. Have a second or even third interview if you need to.

DAY ONE

Congratulations! You've found a great person who has accepted your job offer and you have agreed a start date. In any business, new employees benefit hugely from simple, clear instructions from day one. You're not being kind in letting a new recruit wander aimlessly around the office for their first few days, and nor should you dump too much information on them.

When your new employee starts, tell them exactly what you want them to do, how you want it done and why. Do this, really thoroughly, from the get-go. Invest as much time as you can in them — and you *can* spare the time, however busy you think you are. It will pay dividends for both of you. Make them feel welcome by being friendly and kind, of course. But the biggest kindness you can do, for them and for you, is to make it absolutely clear what is expected of them. Don't pretend to be super laid-back and anything goes if you aren't, and it doesn't, because this will only serve to confuse them at a later date.

It can be a little awkward to spend time with someone new, and there may be a temptation to try and avoid it. But every minute spent with a new colleague is a minute closer to getting to know them, getting them to do the job well and building the foundations for a strong team, so every minute is an investment. And trust me, it's an investment worth making.

CHAPTER 4
LET'S TALK ABOUT TRUST

Now you're beginning to build a team. From now on it's *we*, not me. At the heart of that team lies trust. You need to trust them, and they need to trust you. Why? Well, one reason is that to build a great company, you're going to need to start delegating. And in order to do that, you need to trust that the person you are delegating to will get the job done. Also, if you're going to lead people, they have to want you to lead them. So you have to earn their trust. And that's simple enough. You need to be trustworthy.

It's fascinating how many parents think they can tell their children to do one thing, and then do another themselves. If you tell your child not to swear and then swear like a trooper yourself, you're naive if you think that your child won't hear you and copy you. The same thing applies to trust at work. Don't expect others to follow up on commitments if you don't. Life just doesn't work like that.

So do what you say you will do. Turn up on time. Support your team when they're in difficulty. Never say, 'I'm just being honest,' when, in fact, you're just being rude. You have to mean it — you can't say one thing and do another because people aren't stupid. Behave in a trustworthy way (more on this in Chapter 11) and that trust will grow and develop. So, lead by example because you can be trusted.

LEARN TO DELEGATE

Once trust has been established, you can start to delegate. If you don't, work on the trust some more. Delegation is often seen as weakness. Calling someone a 'really good delegator' is rarely said without cynicism.

But the best leaders are the best delegators, and to develop your team you're going to have to learn how to achieve this. Really, it's about trust and empowerment. If you trust your team, set them free. Give them tasks you would normally do. Let them learn on the job. Then take a step back.

OK, that's easier said than done. The first thing to remember is that clear instructions are paramount here. Take time to explain what you want and do so precisely and in depth. Don't assume that people will understand what's in your head until you tell them.

SET YOUR TEAM FREE

On some levels, I can be a control freak; I suspect many entrepreneurs are built the same way. I have clear, passionately held views on how things need to be done in order for our businesses to move forward. This is good; it's necessary. But in order to be truly efficient, I need to let things go by empowering people around me to get on by themselves. And to achieve this I need to show people how things should be done and then set my team free.

Assuming you've built mutual trust with someone, the

thing to do here is to tell them what you want (remember: clear, simple instructions) and let them get on with it. Let them learn on the job, don't micro manage them and don't interfere. Sometimes things will go horribly wrong, sometimes they will do as good a job as you and sometimes they will do it better.

If it's the former, then gently but firmly correct them. Be clear and precise but don't give up on them. You have to say what is right and you have to explain what's wrong. Do it straight away. Don't baulk at this: praise and criticise with the same directness and kindness that you'd like someone else to show when they speak to you.

So, correct mistakes but be careful not to admonish people who don't approach things in precisely the way you do. One of the magnificent upsides of delegation is that fresh ideas and approaches emerge, and these can be incredibly illuminating. Just because you did something one way doesn't mean that that is the *only* way to do it or, indeed, even the best way. This may bruise the ego a little, but I'm sure you can take it.

With your approval and a little time, the people in your team will become as good as you at a particular task, and then they will become better. And guess what? Once someone else can do those other things, you can then focus on the things you are best at. This is when a team can really start to play to its strengths.

DEALING WITH TRUST ISSUES

I am going to come to conflict resolution and sacking and all of that stuff later. For now, simply follow your gut. Trust is a two-way street. You can do the right thing, but if it's not reciprocated, you need to deal with it.

However tiny or massive your operation might be, if you discover that someone has lied to you or been disingenuous or whatever, then you must deal with it quickly. That said, try to avoid doing anything rashly (and never send grumpy emails at night — sleep on it and review things in the morning). Mull it over, consider things from their point of view, but don't procrastinate and don't be scared to raise the issue with the person in question. It's incredible how many adults shy away from conflict and, in doing so, let a bad situation fester into an awful one. Remember, however unpleasant something seems, once you have confronted and resolved it, it will soon be a distant memory and you can all move on.

Leading and managing other people requires constant effort, learning and reflection. With the different personalities, levels of experience and stress factors, it's a delicate operation. And that's what we're coming onto next.

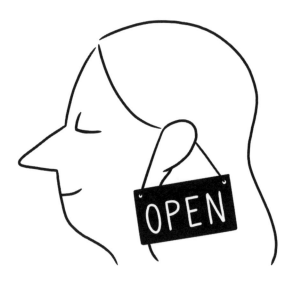

CHAPTER 5
GENTLE LEADERSHIP

However democratic your company or organisation is, someone needs to be in charge. If hierarchy isn't encouraged, a leader will probably emerge anyway. This chapter will show how the most effective leadership is about empathy and kindness. Being loud and bossy never got the best from anyone. The best leaders live at the heart of their teams. They get involved, they ask questions, they listen and hang out. They are part of the team. And from there, good things start to happen.

IT'S GOOD TO TALK

There are plenty of employers who think that they don't have time to chat with their team. They're just too busy and important. But they're wrong. A team is an active community, and showing an interest in that community is a critical part of enabling it to function. In short, you need to know quite a lot about the people in your team in order to get the best from everyone.

Fundamentally, people are interesting. So, sometimes, just try and chat. Don't talk about yourself; ask others about themselves. To some this comes naturally, they just want to learn more about those around them. To others it doesn't come so easily but will start to feel more natural over time.

It's actually rewarding to ask people about their lives and to listen to their responses. But remember to *actually* listen — this isn't about paying lip service. So, concentrate! And you know what? This is easy to do because almost everyone is interesting. You just have to have an open mind and be generous with your questions, and give yourself time to listen and respond.

You might think you don't have much in common with someone, but you just need to scratch the surface. If you discover someone in your team has an unusual hobby, train spotting for example, ask them about it: how many books they've filled with numbers, what *compels* them, how many people share their interest. Spark things up. If they sense that your interest is genuine, they'll share their passion and what they tell you will be interesting. Then later, you can continue that conversation and good things will develop between you, and you will like each other, and from that comes your team.

HAVE EMPATHY

Everyone is someone's child, girlfriend, husband, best friend, grandchild. Remember this. We all have feelings. Everyone is human and has their own network of loved ones and friends outside the office. These things matter at work as much as they matter anywhere else. So, put yourself in someone else's shoes every now and then.

And remember that you are not any more important than anyone else. You may be the founder or the boss or whatever, but everyone is equal. Everyone is special.

To be a great leader you need to know this to be true.

LEAD BY EXAMPLE

Pull, don't push. One of the best ways to help those around you to progress, evolve and blossom in ways that benefit the company is to lead people by example with enthusiasm and energy, rather than pushing them hard.

Positive leadership is rarely about cracking a whip. It's about encouragement and incentive and being a good role model. Sometimes you'll need to lay down the law, but most of the time you just need to lead people by example, so keep yourself, your mood and your actions in check.

THE POWER OF PRAISE

Isn't it funny how we tend to praise children and not adults? Sometimes it feels as if we're praising children every waking minute, in fact. But rarely do we say to a colleague, 'You did something really remarkable there,' or 'You did a much better job than I would have.'

Praise is oxygen, and not just for children. I read somewhere that people would rather have regular praise from their boss than a pay rise. Who knows, but it's not just a way of saying, 'I see you and I hear you,' but rather, 'I *not only* see and hear you, but think you're doing really well.'

There are theories that praise can trigger the same reward centres in the brain — the ventral striatum and ventral prefrontal cortex — that light up during sex. I have no idea if this is true, but I like it so I'm going to run with it. Without necessarily wishing to turn your office into a seething mass of orgasmic positivity, please do consider handing out praise more often. But only do it when you mean it. Done properly and genuinely, praise will help you to build powerful, trust-based relationships with your colleagues. So don't fake it.

BE DECISIVE

If you're a team leader (and remember, it doesn't matter how huge or tiny that team is) you need to make decisions, often on the hoof. Don't be afraid of making decisions; someone has to. Teams cannot operate entirely democratically. So, listen to the views of others, weigh things up, then make a decision and let everyone know the new direction of travel. Decision made! Done.

Don't be scared. You are almost certainly not dealing with absolutes here; there is no right or wrong decision. It's what you do once you've made the decision that counts. Sometimes you don't need advice or *more advice*, you just need a decision. So, make one, risk it, move forward.

Great teams need great leaders, and occasionally leaders need to make difficult decisions and tell people what is expected of them. This is leading from the front and it's what your team expect of you. Follow your gut, even if people disagree with you. Sometimes you will need to be forthright, strong and expressive, but you can still remain polite and considerate. My advice is to make a decision and stand by it.

This gets things done. And however gentle and inclusive your normal style is, being more assertive from time to time will serve you well. People want to look up to — and importantly, respect — a team leader. Remember, you can't please all of the people all of the time.

It took me a long time to understand this. I am a people-pleaser; I want to like people and I want them to like me. This isn't a bad thing; it's good to be sensitive. But it can be exhausting, as well as pointless. These days, as long as I'm doing what I believe to be the right thing for the company as a whole, then I have to stand by those decisions. So, don't mumble, don't procrastinate, don't apologise: make a decision and communicate it effectively.

BE CONSISTENT

Consistency of behaviour is critical to great leadership. Leaders need to be adults, by which I mean balanced, calm grown-ups. Understanding the value of consistent behaviour is half the battle. If you can be consistent in the way you communicate, in how you *are*, it makes it a great deal easier for those who work with you to thrive because they will intuitively begin to understand how things should be done. Which brings me on to moods ...

CONTROL YOURSELF

Given that effective leadership is about leading by example, you need to ensure that you never bring your bad moods into work. Sure, you're going to feel rotten sometimes and have off days. We all do. But as the leader of a team (and that might only be a team of two), you just can't let your moods spill out at work. If you do — and plenty of bosses do — you are simply legitimising moody behaviour in the workplace.

So, learn your moods. Bite your tongue. First, self-awareness. Then self-control.

THE VALUE OF GENTLE, TRUTHFUL ADMONISHMENT

Don't avoid conflict. Remember, if something is wrong, you have to say it is. Without learning how to warn or reprimand someone effectively, you will never build a good team. Mistakes are going to be made and if you don't deal with them, they will probably keep happening. Of course, one option is to revert to doing things yourself. But it's far better to speak to the individual or the team as a whole so they improve.

- **Remember that telling someone else they're wrong doesn't always need to mean that you're right.** What you are trying to do is to get your colleague to see the matter in hand in the same way that you do. It's necessary for your business to work efficiently and move forward.

- **Stay calm.** Breathe, take time out, reflect. Remind yourself you're a really good leader. Calmness is power.

- **When you do correct someone, do it clearly, precisely and in detail.** Don't be smug or self-righteous. Explain precisely why you think what they have done is wrong and how they can correct it.

- **Bring some balance to the conversation.** Maybe even temper this admonishment with praise and encouragement, but don't let the balance shift to the positives just because you don't want to hurt someone's feelings. Be honest and be direct. You owe this to the people on your team to help them to grow and evolve. Be a good teacher.

CHANGING YOUR MIND IS NOT A WEAKNESS

In fact, it's a strength. It's about being open-minded. If you're brave enough to change your mind, then you're on the way to becoming a team leader. Good work!

So many politicians have been vilified by journalists for changing their minds that this has now become known as 'doing a U-turn' and is seen as an entirely bad thing. It isn't. So, allow yourself to change your mind if that's the best course of action — and give your team the freedom to do likewise. This is a natural function of learning and becoming wiser. And it's better to stop a plan now than to linger over something that just doesn't feel right.

GET OVER YOURSELF

At work, as at home, never allow yourself to become isolated. Admit your weaknesses and acknowledge the things you forgot, the things you can't handle. Allow your team to see right into you as often as you can. You are human, and so are they, and this will help build unity.

CHAPTER 6
BETTER COMMUNICATION

Remember that brilliant teacher at school who taught you so well? I hope you had at least one. Maybe you thought you just 'got it' when they were teaching you. But, more likely, they were really good at explaining things — and you felt you could ask a question if anything was unclear.

A team leader (and remember, a team can be two or hundreds or even thousands of people) needs to be a good teacher: precise, patient, sensitive to others' limitations and able to give clear instructions. This chapter is about the importance of good communication, the power of clarity of explanation and the importance of the written word.

EMAIL IS YOUR FRIEND

Email is really useful. It gets a bad rap, but the real enemy is unnecessary group emails, reply-alls or spam — not simple, clear, concise emails that tell everyone what they need to know.

The phone is still a great mode of communication, particularly if you have something complex to discuss and you need to reach an agreement — chances are you will skilfully avoid an incredibly long email thread. But when used properly, the written word is powerful. It is particularly useful when giving instructions, progressing fully developed ideas or when used as a précis to a discussion between a group. Clear instructions are not only a good thing; they are absolutely critical to efficiency. Don't assume that others think the same way that you do, because they probably don't.

And 'just picking up the phone' can be intrusive in ways that email rarely is. Remember that people aren't generally sitting around waiting for you to call them. A call can be a distraction (best leave that to social media). Scheduled phone calls and a follow-up email to clarify points discussed work well.

So, understand the value of emails and *always* read them through before sending. Have you been clear and thorough? Would you understand everything if this was sent to you?

AVOID JARGON

The more clarity you bring to the process of telling people what you need, the more likely it is that things will get done successfully. And that means avoiding jargon, those special 'work' phrases or acronyms that few people understand. Write it as you would say it (and if you speak in jargon, please stop). Jargon is pointless and it doesn't make you any more professional. We have an excellent language that has been developed over millennia. It's the language of Shakespeare and Bennett and it's fine.

LEARN TO VALUE MEETINGS, CONFERENCE CALLS AND AGENDAS ... SERIOUSLY

Your team is going to become a beautiful, well oiled machine and communication is going to be both your engine and your driver. But achieving this isn't all about creativity and flipping open your laptop in hipster coffee shops. It's about the basics: meetings, conference calls and agendas. If you think these are only for boring corporations then you're wrong.

Ignore those who sneer at meetings or say they are a waste of time. They just don't understand how to run them properly. You need meetings in order to communicate efficiently, share ideas with the team and get feedback.

Here are my rules for having a good, efficient meeting:

1. **Start on time, always.**

2. **Limit the time** given to the meeting. Most can be kept within 30 to 45 minutes.

3. **Have an agenda.** You need to know what you want to discuss and achieve.

4. **Have someone steer the meeting.** If the term *chairperson* sounds too stuffy, then fine, call them a *facilitator* or *lead*, but you need someone to move things along and to keep everyone focused.

5. **Try and create an environment** in which those who don't enjoy talking publicly (or indeed at all) feel comfortable contributing.

6. **Leave time for 'Any Other Business'** (AOB). This enables subjects to be raised that maybe didn't make the agenda.

7. **Someone should take notes** then circulate them afterwards with decisions and action points.

HOW TO CHAIR A MEETING

Someone has to lead the meeting, and it might as well be you. Don't feel your meeting needs to resemble an American TV drama with everyone sitting round a table in a featureless room with someone (you) at the head being all bossy. We hold really good meetings in cafés or in front of fires and sometimes we do them walking in the countryside. The rules remain the same though, and if you're the 'chair', it's worth bearing the following guidelines in mind:

1. **Understand** what the team needs to achieve from the meeting.

2. **Let people know** what the meeting is about beforehand.

3. **Be the first to arrive** and have a written agenda. It doesn't need to be too formal. It can even be jotted down on your phone.

4. **Get the meeting started on time.** I'm a stickler for punctuality, so I tend to get going even if people are late.

5. **That said, set a relaxed tone.** Allow for a bit of chat or getting coffee.

6. **Listen.** You may be chairing the meeting, but don't dominate it; perhaps you barely need to talk (see point 7).

7. **Encourage** (but don't force) quiet or reticent people to talk. These people often have the best, most considered ideas, and by encouraging them you are also letting them know they are valued. Be gentle, friendly and non-dismissive.

8. **Take notes**, or make sure someone else does.

9. **Ask questions** so that everyone understands what is being said.

10. **Discourage** side conversations.

Conference calls or Zoom calls (or whatever is the new thing when you read this) are useful too and need to be run in the same way as meetings, which, of course, is what they are.

CLEAR COMMUNICATION IS AS IMPORTANT AS CLEAR PURPOSE

Much of the success of an organisation will come down to the leader's ability to communicate *internally* with the team. Accurate, precise, clear internal communication is vital; without it you can't possibly move in the same direction efficiently. Make sure everyone knows what they are doing and why. Your team will thrive when you're all moving in the same direction with the same ideas.

When you have something important to pass on, try to speak to everyone in your team individually, or at least with as many as you can reasonably manage. Remember, clear and precise: what you say and what people hear are not always the same thing.

In order to achieve this, break down what you are trying to communicate into palatable chunks. Then, once you've spoken to everyone, I suggest that you follow up with a short summary via email reinforcing your key points or instructions.

Don't forget that communicating directly with people makes them feel valued and helps to strengthen relationships.

A lot of good organisations send internal newsletters. The size of the company will have a bearing on whether it's worth the time spent producing one, but when it's done well, with verve and sparkle, it can be a really good idea (less so if it's dull and no one reads it).

GOOD INSTRUCTIONS ARE THE HOLY GRAIL

I'm useless at understanding manufacturer instructions for electrical goods. I just can't seem to *retain* what I'm being told. No, scratch that, generally I can't understand anything *in the first place*. It may well be that there's a part of my brain missing or something. Or maybe these instructions aren't written in a way that everyone can understand! So, here are a few things to remember when issuing instructions.

1. **Use normal everyday language** when writing or speaking. Avoid anything too technical (or jargon!).

2. **Don't assume** the recipient knows everything that you do.

3. **Check** you've been understood before moving on.

4. **Actively listen** to any questions. Answer them patiently and with as much detail as needed.

And finally, some things to avoid if you want to become a better communicator.

1. On email, **don't click 'Reply All'** unless everyone needs to know your response.

2. **Don't email late at night**, especially after a drink.

3. **Don't call or email** someone when you're in a rage. Sleep on it. You'll be much more level-headed in the morning.

4. **Never shout.** Losing your temper takes a long time to recover from.

5. **Watch out** for predictive text and spell-check. Sometimes I read over an email I've written, and certain words have mutated in unimaginable ways. Read before you send.

CHAPTER 7
ENCOURAGING IDEAS

Great ideas are one of the benefits of having other people working with you. To conceive and nurture these ideas you need to create a structure that means the good ones don't go to waste and, equally, the less good ones (as we know, there's no such thing as a bad idea!) are discarded.

IDEAS NEED TO BE CONTROLLED

What do I mean by that? You need to be sure that ideas generated randomly by members of your team don't distract you from other tasks. An idea spurted out by someone while you're in deep concentration is not useful and, importantly, it may well get missed.

So, ask your team to note ideas down. Create a culture whereby members of the team are encouraged to develop ideas themselves before putting them forward. Everyone should follow this process (that includes you) so treat your own ideas as you treat everyone else's.

Then create a proper time for discussion. This could be a weekly ideas meeting, where new ideas and initiatives can be shared and discussed. You need to be open to the fact that the most unexpected people sometimes have the best ideas. Also that those who are customer-facing will have a direct line to what those customers want, so their ideas are usually based on or in response to user feedback. That said, be wary of the sort of comments that suggest 'loads of people have been asking for this' or 'loads of people don't like this'. In this example, you need to quantify what 'loads' means, because it may turn out to just be one grumpy customer.

Within these sessions, make sure everyone is heard. Putting forward a new idea at the risk of it being shot down publicly isn't always easy. Be aware that many people feel vulnerable about speaking up, especially if they are not regarded as the 'ideas person'. Be kind and open-minded, never dismiss things outright, and if an idea really doesn't work for you then explain why.

Occasionally, it is worth developing someone's idea even if it's not the best thing since sliced bread. It will instil confidence in its originator that may lead to more, and often better, ideas, which is good for the team and the company as a whole. Remember that everyone can have good ideas and they will multiply in people if you nurture them. So, give other people's ideas oxygen, even if you're not 100 per cent sure they'll work. Plus, you never know.

Similarly, beware the pitfalls of asking for ideas that you have no intention of implementing. Asking people to spend time coming up with new ideas and initiatives is counter-productive if you are doing so just to appear open-minded.

SOMETIMES YOU NEED
TO PUSH AN IDEA THROUGH

Sometimes you just know that an idea is right, even if other members of the team disagree, and — much like making those difficult decisions — you need to lead from the front.

I once heard a brilliant film director say that he never played 'the power dynamic'. I dislike jargon but I loved the work of this director so I investigated. What he meant was that he never wielded his power simply because he was the boss. But I'm not sure I believe him, because sometimes you do need to implement your ideas simply because you are running the project and have a clear vision of the intended outcome, even if it means spending a bit more time convincing others that it will work! From this single-mindedness can come brilliance.

IMPATIENCE IS A VIRTUE —
IT GETS THINGS DONE

I am wildly impatient and when I was a child my dad would often berate me for being too eager to get things done. In some ways, he was right. As I've grown older, I have come to accept that I may 'suffer' from some sort of mild restless mania. But impatience has its advantages.

Procrastination is the enemy of progress. Don't allow your team to overthink things or spend too long working out every possible scenario. Try out some of these ideas and see if they work. You can always 'do a U-turn' but, most importantly, you need those around you to understand that it's OK to fail. Over the years I have come to realise that I have a weird lack of fear of failure. Maybe this is a characteristic common to many entrepreneurs. I'm pleased to say that I've learned to pass this on to others, albeit in sensible measure.

In short, it's better to have endless ideas that may not work than to have no ideas at all.

MAKING IDEAS HAPPEN (OR NOT)

It's good for morale to encourage your team to try new things. To act, to take some risks, to jump off the edge! But once you have your idea, it's what you do with it that counts. It's how hard you all work on it to bring it to life, how you adapt and evolve it, how you ride the bumps, and importantly, how the team handles failure should that happen.

FAILURE

You and your team have to understand that failure happens and from that we can quickly learn to do things better. Try and avoid berating yourself or others when things go pear-shaped, as they will from time to time. James Joyce saw mistakes as 'the portals to discovery' and I'm completely with him.

You need to show people that not only is failure a vital part of success, but that it's fine, provided they've tried as hard as they possibly can and considered all the alternatives. Many of us don't discuss our own business failures enough, but to do so can be liberating and educational. So, if something doesn't work out then accept it and discuss it with the team so you can all learn from it. Then move on.

This whole process involves vulnerability, stress and maybe even some financial loss, but you must remind those you work with that success is not a simple, straightforward path and it will always involve mistakes. So, lighten up, embrace the failures and let your team know that it's not only normal but necessary.

At these times, be generous. We all need kindness and we all deserve it. Give and receive kindness every single day; it makes the giver feel good and the receiver feel even better. When things haven't worked out, you need to be particularly kind to your team. I'm not talking here about those moments when people have been stupid, lazy or dishonest. I'm talking about when you encouraged an idea (or a way of behaving or thinking) and it didn't bear fruit. You need to let people know that's OK. Your generosity and your consistency in these times will not only act as a powerful tonic to the individual and the whole team, but will reveal itself to be one of the strongest team-binding glues you'll ever encounter.

CHAPTER 8
TOUGH TIMES

Things are going to get tough. I have been through some absolutely brutal times in my working life. Months where I couldn't sleep properly, where suppliers and bank managers were on my case, where my team was buckling. I hope you won't have it as tough as this, but there are always going to be challenging times, caused by external events or internal conflict. But with a solid team in place and careful management, there is no reason why you can't pull through.

In the spring of 2020, I had an interesting 'Guiding the team through tough times' experience. Covid-19 was beginning to raise its murderous head for the first time. It's hard to recall what those days were like, so to refresh your memory, it felt like those moments on a rollercoaster when you're climbing, one ratchet at a time, to the very top before the whole adventure begins. You don't know what lies ahead but you know it's going to be pretty wild, and that you're not going to be able to control it.

A week before he imposed full lockdown, the British Prime Minister told the country not to visit pubs, cafés or restaurants (among other places). This was a bit of a blow to much of the population, but for those of us who owned and ran such businesses (and we ran all three) it was catastrophic. Remember that no financial compensation had been mentioned at this stage; people were just told not to visit.

I was driving home from work when I heard this announcement on the radio and I remember thinking, 'Shit, we have to close everything tomorrow.' I'm an avid consumer of news and it was becoming clear that Covid-19 was coming at us all guns blazing. I called my managing director and told him we had to close, and he agreed.

When I got home, I felt pretty downcast. We'd worked hard on these businesses for 12 years and now we had to close them. I started to run a bath and then it occurred to me: we, as a team, could do something useful, exciting and positive to counter the gloom.

The next morning we had a team meeting. Once we had closed the pub, the restaurant and the café, the idea was to convert the pub into a community shop for the next few weeks. The plan was well received. We started ordering products to sell: meat, veg, household goods, gifts, cards. The tasks were divided up and everyone got to work; we were finding a way to make things work. We installed a coffee machine behind the bar; we baked and cooked; we shifted furniture and lugged fridges; we even got some new uniforms! We hired hand basins for customers, bought industrial tubs of sanitiser and put the pub furniture into storage. People used their own cars and even their bikes. We sent out newsletters, had signs printed and posted on Instagram. In short, a mere 36 hours later, we opened. This wasn't a half-hearted operation; it was a proper shop.

The community responded well. It was particularly beneficial to elderly people or those without cars. But, if I am honest, one of the best outcomes was that it brought the team together during a strange and challenging time.

When so much around them was going pear-shaped, it gave them pride, purpose and positivity. If it had been allowed, we'd have had a big group hug too. The local and even national newspapers came calling. Morning TV was on our case, looking for some good news stories amidst the gloom. And with that, our team stood tall, proud and motivated.

The impact of this project on our team has been profound. We did *that* and we did it *really well*. Its legacy will be lasting on the community, sure, but most importantly on our team. This is the power of leading from the front, of ideas made real, of trust, fearlessness and delegation — and, in particular, of working together towards a common goal.

STAY CALM

When things get difficult, try not to show your fear to the team. You need to share the problems and try to figure out what to do together. But you need to *appear* calm and give the impression that you know how to sort things out, even if you don't *feel* calm at all. This is a vital part of leadership because a team needs to believe in their leader, and if they feel your stress it will impact on them.

Remember to share the problem in a rational, enquiring way. Don't pretend everything is fine if it isn't. So many of us pretend everything is just great in our business when it isn't, which is interesting because a problem shared *is* a problem halved. You'll be amazed by how many times someone, somewhere, has dealt with precisely the same problem. So often there is a solution. You are not alone and it's at times like these that you need your team (and that includes your advisers) to offer up ideas and experience to help the company get through things. For me, this is the very definition of leading from the front. And you can do it.

CONFLICT AND CONCILIATION

Much as unexpected world events are part of life, so is conflict. And it's going to happen in your team. Disagreements will cause stress, hassle and, at worst, serious disruption or financial problems to the business. But how things pan out is largely up to you as team leader. You can deal with it through sensible management and some simple actions.

This section will show you how to manage conflict quickly, efficiently and relatively painlessly. It is not a full, legal manual — not by any stretch. It's a series of hard-learned lessons tempered with advice from the many experts who have taught me along the way.

Before we get into the nitty-gritty, it's worth bearing in mind the following:

First, calmness is power. In any difficult situation, you control how you respond. Breathe deeply, think before you act, and don't panic.

Second, always consider working with a good HR (Human Resources) person. Bigger companies will employ someone full-time, but there are masses of good freelancers available. If you're not sure how to handle a scenario involving someone in your team, consult an HR professional and then you can incorporate their advice with your own approach. But I'd advise against completely ignoring their advice — they tend to know what they're doing.

Third, be careful not to allow yourself to be manipulated by those in conflict. Tread carefully, trust your gut and be wary of any traps you might be walking into.

CONFLICT RESOLUTION

The first lesson here is to deal with conflict quickly. Don't stress about it; very soon it will be nothing but a distant memory. But you do need to nip it in the bud so things don't fester and become far, far worse.

Done well, conflict resolution can offer amazing opportunities for growth within your team. It can build trust and respect. You just need to deal with things properly. In most cases it is actually quite straightforward. Believe it or not, it's one of the few times where you need to behave in the office as you would with children at home.

So let's say two people have a problem and someone needs to take the matter in hand. The quicker the better, especially as the smaller your team, the bigger the impact.

The first thing is to acknowledge that the problem exists, however stupid you think it might be. We are all human and we are all different; no one is absolutely right and no one is absolutely wrong.

I like the word 'conciliation' with all that it implies: mediation, placation, that sort of thing. Handled correctly, it works, and the process will be relatively easy and pain-free.

Once you have acknowledged the problem, you then need to chat with the two people in conflict, separately. It's worth noting here that once you are involved you can't back out. A big advantage of being involved is that it makes people feel seen, heard and valued. Just listening and advising may even sort things out, but, for now, let's assume it doesn't so when you meet, consider the following:

1. **Actively listen to both parties** but try not to take sides. If you do feel you need to take sides, then you'll probably need to move to official sanctions (warnings, sackings, etc.)

2. **Do not say anything** to one person that you won't want to hear repeated back to you when all three parties meet.

3. **Remember** that one, or possibly both, of the parties feel threatened. Let's assume this isn't just an everyday disagreement so it needs to be handled gently.

4. **Explain** how individual perspectives vary and that the situation can be resolved, if both parties want it to be. Urge conciliation.

It's no good just hoping for the best. So, like it or not, once you've spoken to them both separately you need to get them together in a private, relaxed space. Give plenty of advance warning so both can mentally prepare. Next, follow this process.

1. **Be present** but let them do most of the talking. You can help them to sort this. But remember, it's not about you; it's about them.

2. **Give both sides time** to explain their issue without interruption. Remember that often the conflict will be about feelings as much as anything.

3. **Stay calm.**

4. **Remind them** of the life-changing magic of getting along with each other. Grievances, grudges, resentments and arguments are time-wasting distractions.

5. **Offer alternative solutions.** Either we do this, or we do that. But, either way, something needs to change.

6. **Try to settle** on a way of resolving the issue that is broadly acceptable to both parties. You may have to be quite tough here.

7. **Write the agreement down** and send a copy to each of them. Keep a record and send a copy to your HR person if you have one.

8. **Follow this all up** with another meeting, say within a week, to review how things are going.

Of course, there will be times when you just won't get two people to agree, or there will be no common ground. If that's the case then you're going to have to make a decision and come down on one side of the argument. In a nutshell, this process is about simple, clear, strong, fair communication, as well as empathy, kindness and humanity.

SACKING AND REDUNDANCY

First up, the bad news: unpleasant things will happen. At some time or another, you will need to sack someone and you will need to make someone redundant. Remember that in the long term, this may benefit the whole team.

Assuming you have a contract in place with your employee, there are legal processes to follow here and they vary from one situation to another. There is a system of warnings, follow-ups and final letters. I'd suggest consulting an expert in this area so you know exactly what the process is and what you need to do to ensure everything is done correctly.

Just so we're clear, my advice in this book is not about legal matters because I'm not a lawyer; it's about humanity and leadership. It's pretty much the same whether you are dealing with sackings or redundancy. So remember my caveat: you may well need proper HR or legal advice. I don't say this to protect myself, but rather to protect you and your colleagues.

First, some personal stuff. Act on this in conjunction with the more technical bits on the next page.

- You're in an unpleasant situation but you need to act. Don't delay and bury your head in the sand.

- If you handle it quickly and do so properly, you are going to make things better for everyone on your team.

- Do the dirty work yourself. Don't be a wimp.

- Remember empathy! Everyone is someone's brother, sister, husband, partner, grandparent, and so on. Everyone deserves kindness and consideration. So be kind but be direct.

- Look the person in the eyes, breathe deeply, speak slowly.

- Try to part on reasonable terms.

- Explain to your team why you are doing this and exactly what you are doing.

Now, the good news: you can resolve the matter at hand if you remember those personal things and follow the more technical guidelines below.

- You will need to develop a fair and consistent policy on sackings and redundancies, however small your company is. Write it down. Get to know it.

- You need to have a fair disciplinary process in place. It isn't only your opinion that counts — others such as an HR person, senior colleagues or a lawyer must have input here.

- Note down any evidence that you intend to draw on when reprimanding or firing someone. You need to back up decisions with facts and real clarity.

- You must seek professional advice.

- You must give warnings of meetings well in advance to allow both sides time to prepare.

- In difficult meetings, encourage the attendee to bring someone with them to act as a witness. This will benefit both parties.

- Write up notes on what has been said in these meetings and make sure everyone has a copy. Make sure both parties agree that the notes are an accurate reflection of what was said and agreed by initialing or signing them.

- Good luck.

STRESS

In the last part of this chapter, we'll look at the stress you might be under, but first we'll deal with the stress others might be under. And if you think that sounds odd, I've got some bad news for you ...

OTHER PEOPLE'S STRESS IS YOUR PROBLEM

This is unfortunate but I'm afraid it's true. I'm not going to get too deep here, but people in your team will suffer from stress. This may cause them to be unproductive and even unpleasant, and you're going to have to deal with it.

The key thing is to learn to recognise how stress manifests itself and to encourage an open-minded approach to it. It happens, it's fine, it's normal. But taking a couple of days off to deal with acute stress is usually not enough. When I was going through a particularly stressful period, I found cognitive therapy very useful (my doctor recommended a great person). I went to a private consultant and it was money well spent. But there is a mass of help available. Depending on the level of stress involved, and possible causes, you may wish to encourage individuals in your team to seek help if they are struggling. Don't forget, everyone's stress thresholds are different. And don't be dismissive; stress is real and it's your job to help those people in your team to manage it.

I learned a great deal about helping people with stress during 2020 and 2021 when, at one time or other, it seemed that everyone in my teams suffered with it for all sorts of understandable reasons.

Of course, it is often hard to distinguish between stress that you can directly help with (work-related issues) and that which has its roots elsewhere (stuff that is going on outside of work) and may be out of your control. But, either way, you need to get involved, to at least try to make things better, even if it's just lending an ear.

If you think the stress has something to do with work, then you may be able to help in practical ways. First, listen to problems. Often just being heard is enough to relieve some of the anxiety. Second, offer up some solutions. This might be as simple as sharing workload or helping with time management. It might be more complicated and involve offering your colleague some training to help them develop or learn specific skills.

The important thing is to listen and then to take the matter seriously by offering solutions — or as I've said, simply listening can be hugely beneficial. This will build a happier team. Remember that to be stressed is to be human. As a team leader, your job is to accept that people will have difficult times. And really, that's already half the battle.

BUT WHAT ABOUT YOUR OWN STRESS?

This is harder. I can say, hand on heart, that I am writing from experience here. I have closed businesses, I have been unable to sleep for weeks and I have developed stress rashes across my face. I have been *super*-stressed.

From time to time, things are going to be tough. In fact, there will be disasters. You cannot let your stress affect your decisions or behaviour at work. You're going to have to find a way to deal with it.

As I've already said, a problem shared is often a problem halved, maybe even solved. Discussing certain issues with your mentor or other experts in a calm, rational way is the best way of solving problems and, in so doing, relieving stress. A nurturing professional relationship can be really helpful. Don't let the fear build up. If you can't pay a tax bill, call the tax people. If you keep losing money despite making good sales, call your mentor. Speak to your partner or sibling. I don't mind who, just talk to someone.

But — there's always a 'but', isn't there? — when things are tough, you will sometimes need to *pretend* to your team that you are fine and in control when you actually feel completely the opposite. Why? Because you're a leader and people will take their cues from you. If you seem to be melting under the weight of stress, then they will too. It's that thing they say about horses (correctly, in my limited experience): the horse can sense when the rider is panicked, and they behave accordingly. And that doesn't help anyone at all. You can let it all out in the car on the way home, but leadership is sometimes about seeming to be in control when that's the last thing you feel.

I write more about looking after yourself in the final chapter, but for now, consider running. A good run kills stress, dead. I am a committed runner and have been for around forty years (and yes, my knees are fine, thanks).

Nowadays, I try to do one longish run at the end of each summer to give myself a goal, with smaller runs leading up to it. Of course, not everyone can run, but if you can walk reasonably well, you can run. You can! Start small and build slowly. Rest on as many days as you run. Be prepared for periods of no progress or for setbacks. But keep at it. Running is simple and cheap. It lifts you up, clears your mind and offers up deep euphoria, solutions and perspective. As the phrase goes: 'Running enables the mind to run the body and not the body run the mind.' And although it's hard, isn't everything that's worth achieving?

And, while I'm on the subject, running offers one particular life lesson, and it's this: concentrate on what you know you can do. One step at a time. All you can do is move forward. Just focus on that and momentum will follow. Oh, and getting out of the front door is the hardest part of any run.

Most runners run not because they want to live longer, but because they want to live life to the fullest.

Haruki Murakami, *What I Talk About When I Talk About Running*

CHAPTER 9
THE HUDDLE

Football. I love it. My dad first took me to Anfield football stadium to see Liverpool play when I was seven, and I have been hooked ever since.

Back in the 1970s, when I first went with Dad, the great Bill Shankly was manager. He was a true leader, passionately committed to the club and the wider city. A clever, generous, spirited, hard-working man who did what he said he would. He was not only massively successful but widely respected. Everyone in the club's community loved Shankly. He understood that the stadium cleaners were as important as the superstar strikers who were as important as the fan in the stands. He understood that unity, and its attendant success, come from common purpose. And that the best way to communicate common purpose is to lead by example.

At the time of writing, we have Jürgen Klopp at Liverpool — probably the club's most successful manager since Shankly. Klopp is loved throughout the world for his intellect, his generosity and his work ethic. His heart is worn on his sleeve and his self-effacing humour is as unusual as it is inspiring. He knows that unity builds success and, like Shankly, that leading by example is the most powerful tool we have. Not only that, Klopp also values the person who looks after the players' kit as much as his captain. Everyone knows him, and he takes the time to know them in return, and that creates a powerful, unbeatable momentum.

But there are two more things that unite these men. And it isn't about being Mr Nice Guy.

Shankly and Klopp share a deeply competitive gene, the absolute will to win. No, scratch that, the *need* to win. We are talking about deeply rooted and unavoidable competitiveness. While it's OK being the good guy much of the time, sometimes for you to win, you have to see everyone else as the enemy, to understand the deep power of setting your team against everyone else. From time to time, it's got to be them against us.

This doesn't just apply to competitive sport. It exists in the music industry too. Remember The Smiths, The Clash, Public Enemy? The best bands are gangs. Gangs with a common purpose, world domination in their sights, unity, a uniform, a language. It's a pre-gig dressing room with no visitors allowed. A group bow at the end of the show. It's us, and only us.

The Clash were masters of this. From the very beginning they knew they were world-beaters, but that success was up to them alone. Conquering the world meant going into battle.

So how does this relate to your team? I call this *The Huddle*. It's the core group in a circle before the big game or the gig at Shea Stadium. It's that unbreakable gang with a common purpose, a group mentality, an understanding of the fight ahead. A spirit so raw and powerful that it makes others jealous, gains momentum and pushes you forward to win.

BE MORE JÜRGEN KLOPP

Many of Klopp's team-building techniques won't suit your team or personal style, but some will. As the man himself says, 'You can speak about spirit or you can live it.' To prove his point, he once took his Mainz football team to a Swedish lake for five days where there was no electricity and they all had to catch their own food from the lake. Similarly, after one particularly poor first-half performance, instead of shouting and screaming he just said to his players at the interval, 'Since we're here we might as well play football.' Humour and self-awareness go a long way. This is going to be hard, but it will also be fun.

BE MORE LIKE THE CLASH

The greatest rock and roll band ever? Maybe. The last gang in town? Definitely. They dressed like a gang, thought like one, walked like one. They knew they were the best, no argument. Here's Joe Strummer, the singer:

'It was us against the world. We weren't parochial, we weren't narrow-minded Little Englanders. We had the suss to embrace what we were presented with, which was the world.'

And lo and behold, world domination!

HOW TO HUDDLE

Here are a few tips to help create that huddle spirit within your team. Chances are you're competing in an established industry where corporate giants run the show. You're going to need courage, to be fearless and show some fighting spirit.

COMMON PURPOSE

Everyone, insiders and outsiders, needs to know what you are aiming for. What does 'winning' look like to you? Have some long-term objectives in mind. Write them down and share them with the team. Talk about how you're going to get there.

PHYSICAL CONTACT IS GOOD

Team handshakes, high fives and hugs will help everyone (unless there's a global pandemic underway).

REMIND THEM THAT THEY'RE THE BEST

A bit of hubris never hurts. Your team can do anything it wants to. Show everyone in your team that they are valued.

IF YOU AREN'T THE BEST, SOMEONE ELSE WILL BE

It's true! If you don't win, someone else will. Oh, and the better you become at things, the more others will try to outmanoeuvre you. Try and stay ahead of the game.

STEP OUT OF YOUR COMFORT ZONE

You know that fridge magnet that says, 'Do one thing every day that scares you?' There is some truth in it. Push yourself, push others. From this come unity and strength. The best thing that one of my teams did was a group Tough Mudder (a muddy, challenging, grown-up obstacle course). It was brutal for many of the gang but, as a team, they never looked back.

BE MORE GENEROUS THAN ANYONE ELSE

Why not? If you pay better, praise better and chat better, you'll build a better team. A more long-lasting, high-achieving and loyal one that will always beat the opposition.

DO STUFF TOGETHER

You don't hear about 'team building' much these days but a trip away from the office doesn't need to cost much money, and it can rapidly build unity and togetherness. Make sure you organise them well. It doesn't need to be complicated. The best thing we did recently was cook and eat supper together.

HAVE FUN

Create a cheerful place to work. Good businesses actively encourage workplace chat. Tease affectionately, joke and laugh at yourself. Eat together. Karaoke, anyone?

You want to be the best, don't you? If not, what's the point?

**For everything to stay the same,
everything must change.**

Giuseppe Tomasi di Lampedusa, *The Leopard*

CHAPTER 10
EMBRACING CHANGE

If you haven't read *The Leopard*, then I urge you to do so. Set largely in the 1860s, it's a short, wonderful novel about mortality, imperfection and change. And at the very beginning sits that phrase: 'For everything to stay the same, everything must change.'

This is not, as it may first appear, paradoxical nonsense. It states the blindingly obvious: that every organisation, every family, every group of people needs to be open to change, to evolve and adapt. You must encourage change at work, whatever your role.

INERTIA IS SLOW DEATH

One of the best things about working in small companies or departments is that you and your team can adapt quickly. You are nimble and you are free to make mistakes as you evolve.

If you want a snapshot of a world without change then think back to the dawn of music streaming. A time when the record companies spent years fighting Napster to stop them from reinventing the way people consumed music.

Instead of adapting to embrace technology and new ideas, record companies thought they could protect their well-established practices by throwing huge sums of money and endless energy at fighting the streaming companies. And while they were concentrating on trying to eliminate Napster, along came Apple, Spotify and their friends, who stole massive chunks of market share. Or, in more everyday terms, imagine a world where teenage children still go to bed at the same time as before they went to primary school. These are worlds without change.

ENCOURAGE CHANGE EVERY DAY

Sometimes change happens and there's nothing you can do about it other than respond as best you can. Just look at the events of 2020 and 2021. But sometimes, you need to actively bring the change yourself. Here's how you do it.

- **Acknowledge that people are often scared of change.** It takes them away from comfort and normality, from things they know and understand. And, however bold or entrepreneurial *you* might be, you'll need to respect this very understandable human emotion to make progress.

- **Explain what happens when you don't change.** Maybe tell the story about Napster. Remind people that although it can, at first glance, appear scary, it can also be really exciting: new friends, falling in love, a new home, a new discovery. These are all good things.

- **It's that thing about communication again.** If you're going to initiate change, to mix things up a bit, you'll need to explain things clearly so no one feels left behind or frightened. Moreover, you want to include people in the many positive aspects of change so that everyone feels part of your collective success.

- **This is the absolute key: you need to create a culture where there is no fear of failure.** The best way to do this is to make change a gradual, *everyday* thing. You need to encourage a constant process of evolution through small steps so that when things go wrong in this process, they aren't too massive to be undone. Small steps, every day. Forward momentum. Slowly but surely.

- **Make sure you never berate someone for making a change that goes wrong**, provided that the intention was to move forward. But don't allow retrogressive change — some people love to move backwards. Don't tolerate that!

- **Encourage change even when it might not seem necessary**, otherwise you risk allowing your organisation to fall into what is known as 'learned helplessness'. In a nutshell, this is the situation where we wait for others to help us because we feel we aren't allowed to, or can't, try things ourselves. This is the sort of thing that happens to huge departments in the civil service, for example. People *can't* change because they are waiting for the impetus to do so from above, and that never comes because the organisation is just too big and too set in its ways. Do not become that organisation.

- **Procrastination is the enemy of progress.** Don't overthink things and don't allow others in your team to overthink things. This is easy if the changes are gradual, if they are seen as attempts to make things better and not as absolute, irreversible alterations. Make a decision and try things out. Questions will usually answer themselves. You'll soon know if it's right or wrong and, if it's the latter, you can try something else.

- **Impatience is a virtue.** It gets things done. As I mentioned in the Chapter 7, I am impatient, and sometimes that's bad. It can be really annoying for people that I work with; I want stuff done unreasonably quickly. As a child I was always told to be more patient — mainly, I think, because I wasn't good at things that needed me to follow detailed instructions. As an adult, though, I often come across things that have no instructions and it's precisely that lack of patience that helps me to make progress. I just get on with stuff, making it up as I go along, and on the whole it works pretty well. So, encourage your team to get on with things. To try them without fear of retribution if it doesn't quite work out as planned. That way they continue to learn on the job. Procrastination and too much discussion are the enemies of progress. Do it! It's right in front of you. (Maybe it's no coincidence I'm writing a *Do* book.)

If you evolve as a company through new ideas and their implementation, then your team really will start to thrive. There is energy and momentum in change. People want to be challenged, and with each small success (and, yes, small failures too) they grow. Follow this advice and you will empower people and they will, in turn, build resilience within your company.

CHAPTER 11
HOW TO BEHAVE

Teams need guidance on how to behave and that guidance stems from your company values and purpose (which I mentioned in Chapter 2). This chapter is about your team's behaviour, about what to do to create a happy, productive, energised and positive team. To get the best from everyone, of course, you need to lead from the front, to do exactly what you want others to do — and this includes how to behave.

GOSSIP

This is a good place to start. Most gossip is harmless on many levels, but to know you are being gossiped about can be unsettling and it can often be upsetting. It doesn't matter what the intention of that gossip is (and its intention is often benign); it's how it is received that matters, how it feels to the person who's being gossiped about.

Gossip is generally negative, intrusive and inaccurate, so it should be discouraged in the workplace. And it's a waste of time. So, don't listen to conjecture or rumour and resist the temptation to pass it on. Make it clear that it has no place in your team.

(Of course, sometimes you can gossip about the opposition. I'm sure Jürgen Klopp would encourage that!)

ANECDOTE

This isn't the same thing as gossip but this is a good place to address it. Do not make decisions based on anecdote. There's often a temptation to do this in small customer-facing operations: 'loads of people are asking for us to bring back this style of jumper' or whatever. Well, you know what 'loads of people' means. Just don't make decisions based on hearsay. Make them on clear evidence or your gut, but not something that someone heard someone else say to someone else.

MANNERS

Now we're getting to it. Good manners. Manners get a bad rap: they're old-fashioned and designed to control people or whatever.

But I have a feeling that we're actually talking about 'etiquette' when we dismiss manners. Most people indulge in etiquette, even though they might not know it. That it's not right to use your knife in your left hand or have a coloured tattoo; these are the tiny indicators by which we choose our tribe, by which we *identify* ourselves. Etiquette is fine; I mean, it's a bit stupid, but it doesn't hurt anyone.

Manners, I think, are more basic. They are the code by which we react to those around us and, as such, they matter.

When it comes to how you and your team behave publicly, then good manners really do matter. People notice and appreciate them. It doesn't cost anything to smile and say 'hello', to say 'please' and 'thank you'. It may sound obvious, but you're not that person who ignores the waiter when they deliver your food, are you? Thank people regularly, with your eyes, like you mean it.

So, treat everyone that you encounter in the same civilised way, and expect your team to do the same whether you're there or not.

You may need to outline what behaviour is expected of your team. They are ambassadors for your company in everything they do. You'll need to keep an eye on this stuff and flag it when individuals get it wrong. Like so much in this book, it's an ongoing process, not a series of rules you lay down and leave alone. Again, the best way to instil this in your team is to lead by example. You talk the talk, so you've got to walk the walk. And this needs to happen on good days and bad. Consistency is key. You are no more busy or important or tired or rushed than anyone else. Here are a few useful reminders:

- **Do what you say you'll do, when you say you'll do it.** Always. And if you don't, don't expect others to. If you can't meet deadlines or whatever, tell people.

- **Be punctual.** Always. It's not difficult. If you think it is, get over yourself and make more effort.

- **Answer emails.** You don't have to do it immediately and it doesn't have to be an elaborate reply. But I'm sure you notice when an email of yours goes unanswered.

- **Return calls.** Again, this doesn't have to be straight away. If things are busy, then make a note to call them back. Otherwise, have someone who answers the phone who can separate the wheat from the chaff and will tell the caller that you aren't able to deal with this at the moment.

- **Listen.** Listen to what is being said and listen to what is being implied. It's polite, but it's also sensible. Progress comes through listening.

- **Make time for conversation.** It's a good thing (provided it doesn't become gossip). Good teams are communities and need to get to know each other. Conversation is not a waste of office time. Friends at work get stuff done together.

- **Make people go home at a sensible time.** Enough is enough. You are going to have to work unbelievably hard to succeed. But please send people home at a sensible time each evening, and don't make them start stupidly early either. Oh, and everyone should take a lunch break.

- **Make all guests feel welcome.** This especially applies to young people and those pitching for work, those that may be nervous, those for whom this meeting might be a really big deal.

- **Encourage stupidity and fun.** Laughter brings people together like little else.

CHAPTER 12
THE POWER OF (VERY) SMALL TEAMS

It's true: two people can be a legitimate team. Running a business or organisation, no matter the size, is going to be a lot easier if you work alongside someone. This chapter will cover working with a business partner; working with someone you have a personal relationship with (a romantic partner or family member); and finally, working with a second-in-command. There are lots of similarities in the lessons that need to be applied, but each merits its own section.

WORKING WITH A BUSINESS PARTNER

Hire someone you like, but remember that you don't have to be best friends. They don't have to like the same things as you or hang out with the same people. In fact, it's probably better if they don't. Choose someone with complementary skills and let them get on with it. Let them challenge you. An accountant and a creative are a great combination, as are a visionary and someone with operational skills. All of the best business partnerships are constructed like this. Remember that no two people are the same and that is precisely why you're working with them.

Here are a few thoughts on working with a business partner:

You need to respect the person you choose, because you are going to have to trust them with *everything*. This will be at the root of your success. But you'll only achieve it if you let them do their stuff without interference.

Be happy to share any spoils equally with this partner from the start. Pay them what you pay yourself. If they haven't invested in the company, offer them share options (a benefit in the form of the ability to purchase shares at a discounted price, generally offered if they help you to meet certain targets). Remember that 50 per cent of a great company is worth more than 100 per cent of a second-rate one.

Have a written agreement in place reflecting your financial agreement, as well as an employment contract. You might think everything will be fine but if things go wrong, you'll need a clear (legal) framework to deal with issues and disputes.

Communicate your desires, aims and needs clearly in conversation and in writing. Do this right at the beginning. You both need to be moving in the same direction at all times. Make sure that you both fully agree on your various purposes (see Chapter 2).

Draw up boundaries right at the beginning: no calls at the weekend, no email after 8pm, that sort of thing. Agree that you are going to stick to these.

Put rules in place that guide you when you disagree: a few basic rules, some processes. These are useful things. Sometimes you will have disagreements. In the meantime, agree to speak freely and listen carefully, and always with consideration.

Never undermine your partner in front of anyone else in the team. You need to appear absolutely unified even when you're annoyed with each other.

Always ensure that your partner is consulted on those matters within their area of expertise. If you're a creative and you work with an accountant, then don't make financial decisions without them.

Don't double up on tasks. Trust them to do their job and they'll trust you to do yours. Don't do everything together.

Avoid anything even approaching co-dependency: your business partner is not responsible for your emotional needs or your self-esteem. Don't expect them to tell you how great you are.

WORKING WITH YOUR OTHER HALF

This is complicated and interesting. I am talking about your husband, wife, girlfriend, boyfriend, best friend — that sort of person. There's probably a whole book in this but I will compress it into a few short chunks of hard-learned lessons.

My wife Caroline and I have worked together for around thirty years and for a time we really struggled with it. For many years we had young children, we ran small businesses and our office was at home. It was unbelievably hard and, if I am honest, I am not sure how we survived it. But we did. Now, after a great deal of learning and adapting, we're pretty good at it. So, this is how we've made it work:

First, remember you chose your partner. That decision has already been made. I can't help with that. For simplicity's sake, I am going to focus on working with your romantic partner. But the rules are pretty much the same for anyone you have an existing, close personal relationship with. First things first: working together and being together are not the same thing. This is much harder than working with someone who is solely a business partner.

Proceed with caution, whether you have only recently met or been together for ages. This new business relationship will put immense strain on your personal relationship. Just because you make a good team in one way, it doesn't mean you will in another. The idea of doing *everything* together and riding off into the sunset at retirement, still holding hands, with a successful business tucked under your belts, is almost certainly fantasy.

Success in your relationship at work is based on pretty much the same principles as success in your relationship at home. In order to make things operate smoothly in your work life together, you need a few rules and guidelines, just like you do in your home life.

Don't get all tied up in the romance of it all. This is going to be tough. It will be great if you make it great, but could be a disaster if you don't. It's vital to discuss and agree everything before you start, however tempting it is to just muddle along and see how things go. It's much easier to set the rules before the pressure starts to mount. Here are a few suggested guidelines:

- **Respect is at the root of this.** You need to show your partner the same respect at work as you do at home. Do not patronise, don't be bossy and never shout. Never, ever, allow yourself to be a grumpy sod at work; you must remain professional.

- **Allow your other half to keep your ideas in check.** Don't be defensive. If you're a good balance to one another at home, then it follows that you'll be the same at work.

- **Set boundaries for when you do and don't work.** Give yourselves a cut-off time in the evening. Avoid work talk on Sundays and in bed. The rules you make will depend on the dynamic of your relationship, but you need a clear time frame that you are both comfortable with.

- **Try to have an office in a separate building.** For many years we had an office in the house, and it was just too close to our kitchen and with it our home life. I found it hard to understand when we were at home and when we were at work. A shed is fine, but a proper, remote space that you have to travel to is best. Ideally you would contain work conversation to that space too, then once you leave, you leave.

- **Continually check** that you both have the same aims, the same levels of commitment and the same targets for the business.

- **Define your roles really carefully and stick to them.** If you trust your partner with a role, trust their decisions. In terms of myself and Caroline, this has been our clearest success both at home and at work. I don't interfere with her tasks, and she doesn't interfere with mine. Of course, the more we just get on with things, uninterrupted, the better we become at them. Win win.

- **As with other best practice for teams, have formal meetings** and treat them as you would any other meeting (see Chapter 6). Communicate clearly, if necessary in writing. Don't swat each other's ideas aside or be dismissive.

- **Make sure you both agree how the finances work.** I'd recommend using an external accountant.

- **Listen to each other's needs.** Just because you feel like chatting business on a Saturday (even if that is one of your agreed times), it doesn't mean your partner does. Be sensitive. A task you feel passionate about may not hold the same weight for your other half.

- **Take holidays** where you avoid work for most of the day. I also strongly recommend days or long weekends where you do things entirely apart from one another.

- **Avoid either overt displays of affection or arguments in front of others**, especially other members of your team. I'm not sure which is worse; neither is good.

- **Remember that your friends might not be as gripped** by the minutiae of your business life as you two are. Don't be boring.

- **You are going to need to create an open and honest way of discussing things** that one or other of you doesn't feel are right. This is just the same as you'd need to do with any team member, but fraught with potential upset.

- **Finally, make sure that you continue to have fun** and that you work harder on your relationship than you do on your business. Seriously, at the end of it all the thing that really matters is you two. Business can be fleeting and, ultimately, pretty pointless compared to what you have together.

While all this might seem a bit formal and off-putting, I should just say that working together can be absolute magic. You just need to tread cautiously and remember the rules.

WORKING WITH A SECOND-IN-COMMAND

This isn't quite the same as a business partner or your other half. It applies if the other person is subordinate to you — a deputy, if you will. Here is some guidance that is very specific to this role.

- **Choose a second-in-command who absolutely gets what you do and shares your values**: how you treat people, what you believe in, what sort of conduct is expected within your team, what your aims are. The other bits of their job can be learned in due course.

- **Go with your gut instinct.** Only you will know if they're the right person for you.

- **This person must be capable of challenging you.** And their ability to do this is largely up to you. Let them question your decisions. Listen to what they say. Just because you're the boss, it doesn't mean that what you say is always right.

- **Don't become close friends.** This is a tough one, as you will be working closely together. However, there is a hierarchy here and you need to learn to keep your distance. This is something that you'll encounter a lot as you lead: the need to be friendly while avoiding becoming friends with your team. Why? Because emotional distance is critical to issuing instructions that you expect to be followed, particularly if those are tough instructions. You need the sort of respect that emotional distance brings. Which brings me to ...

- **Remember that you have to be able to issue corrections to this person.** If you become too close you won't be able to do this, and the relationship won't function properly.

- **Never undermine your second-in-command** by letting your team ask you for decisions that should be made by them. Never, ever, criticise your second in front of the team.

- **Equally, never issue instructions** that should be dealt with by your second. Let them do their job.

- **Use this person!** Speak often, communicate decisions through clear explanation, write instructions and have formal meetings. They are there to help you and will probably be the most important member of your team.

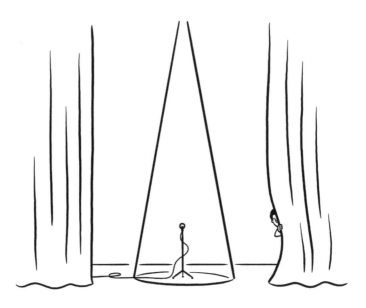

CHAPTER 13
TEAM BUILDING FOR INTROVERTS

Traditionally, leading a team is seen as something that's best done by an extrovert, and maybe most team leaders *are* more likely to be extroverts than introverts. But there is no reason why someone who has a more introverted nature can't be an incredible team leader and get the absolute best from their teams.

Team building is about quiet, considered, mature action rather than big shouty statements. There is an argument that introverts — being, perhaps, deeper thinkers, more considered, sensitive, even more thoughtful than extroverts — can create better teams.

Think about it. What makes a good team leader? Well, it certainly isn't a show-off or the person who shouts loudest or loves the sound of their own voice. It's someone who inspires others through their actions, who knows their job, who's honest, sensitive and kind, who cares about people and is prepared to take it on the chin for them. Someone who's hard-working and generous, who has an idea and knows how to communicate it. It's an innovator who's good with people and always remains level-headed. It's all of this and more. So, in a nutshell, it has very little to do with being the noisy one at the back of the bus and much more to do with intelligence, sensitivity and spirit. Remember, *The Apprentice* is entertainment; life is not like that.

The guidance and advice in this book are aimed at all sorts of people, and if you are more introverted, that certainly doesn't exclude you. Having said that, here are a few specific tips that might be useful if you're naturally that way inclined or have any doubts about rising to this challenge:

- **Know your strengths.** You are really very good at plenty of things. Be yourself. Be genuine. You don't need to pretend to be something you're not. You don't have to be the gregarious person with all the jokes.

- **Explain to people** that you don't find some of this stuff easy. As always, it's about communication. Don't overthink this side of your character. Leadership and team building are about a million different things. Having charisma and being introverted are not mutually exclusive by any means.

- **Introverts often hold their thoughts internally** for longer than extroverts. If you do this, make sure that your team know that this is how you work. Communicate!

- **But how do you communicate** your excellent thoughts and ideas if speaking to groups is something that doesn't come easily? You can, of course, communicate ideas in writing. As I've already mentioned, sending a clearly written email is often the most effective way of communicating. Of course, there will be times when you have to communicate verbally. Try doing it sitting

down, behind a table or with small groups initially.
It's always a good idea to rehearse what you want to say.
It does, in fact, become easier every time you do it.

- **Always have meetings with small groups.** This may
  mean you need more meetings, but short meetings are
  the answer to an efficient life anyway, so focus on that
  and you'll get plenty done.

- **Don't be ashamed to admit** that you don't enjoy public
  speaking. This is actually a great technique for getting
  people on your side.

- **Allow yourself plenty of time alone.** You'll know what
  the best balance is for you, but perhaps give yourself
  30 minutes alone for every hour that you're with the
  team. Use this time to think, process and recharge.

CHAPTER 14
RESPECT YOURSELF

So much of this book is about respect. Respect for others —your co-workers, the person doing deliveries, the tax people, your accountant, indeed everyone you encounter. But, whatever you do, don't forget to respect *yourself*. If you don't look after yourself, you haven't got a hope of making it all work, and that will impact negatively on the entire team.

In the 30+ years that I've been building teams, this is something that I've frequently forgotten. The result? Personal mayhem. Sleepless nights, anxiety, physical illness, a back so stiff I can barely walk. I've put everything and everyone else ahead of myself, which is not a good way to go about things. Today I am getting better at looking after myself, but it's still two steps forward, one step back.

So, I've learned a few things along the way. And as we come to the end of this book, I thought it might be useful to share them with you. The life lessons that follow aren't about big dramatic moments. You need to apply them every day: when things are going well, and when they aren't.

LESSON 1:
BE ORGANISED

Chaos is debilitating, exhausting, time-consuming, stressful, pointless and entirely avoidable. Work at becoming more organised. It's a game changer. I used to be pretty chaotic, losing things, never quite getting around to filing, making lists on envelopes, and so on. These days I'm incredibly well organised and, as a result, am far more productive, calm and efficient. So be rigorous with lists, filing and putting things away in the right place. Work at it every day.

LESSON 2:
YOU ARE NOT A SUPERHERO

You need time out. You need to switch off. You must leave your phone alone from time to time. You don't need to be on call all of the time. There are no medals for the person who works the longest hours. Some time ago I switched off all social-network notifications and I stopped taking my phone into the bedroom. This has really helped me.

LESSON 3:
YOU NEED A HOBBY THAT CONSUMES YOU

'Hobby' is an old-fashioned word but it's a good one. A good hobby uses your brain and maybe your hands and, when you're fully absorbed in it, is a profound act of meditation. (The idea of a 'businessy' side project is a good one, but not the same as a hobby.)

I have a few hobbies but the biggest one is music. I listen to endless music (I have a truly vast record collection), read about it, watch and listen to documentaries about it, and go to live performances as often as I can. It's a complete escape, deeply consuming and a potent reminder that art is as vital as oxygen.

Do something you really love that's unrelated to work: make something, learn something, take yourself right away from everything. Get in the flow zone — the meditative, often transcendental state of being that you achieve when you're completely absorbed in what you're doing. It's great. All that matters is that you love it, then its impact will be immense.

LESSON 4:
EXERCISE IS POWER

Make it part of your life, and the rewards will keep on coming. If you've read Chapter 8, then you'll know that running is my thing. But it doesn't matter what you do, just stretch, breathe, sweat and enjoy the endorphins.

LESSON 5:
READ AS MUCH AS YOU CAN AND MAKE ROOM FOR NOVELS

Reading a novel will teach you more about the world around you than anything else you might choose to read. The novel is possibly the greatest art form. Don't ignore it. At their best, novels offer portals into other worlds and insight into the human condition in ways that nothing else can. Novels are power. They will give you power. And, what's more, because storytelling is at the root of all marketing, reading novels will help you tell better stories.

LESSON 6:
REMEMBER THE GOOD THINGS

When you wake in the middle of the night and your brain is chucking all sorts of bonkers worries at you that are driving you nuts, try thinking about GOOD things. To begin with, I suggest that you match every bad thought with one good one, however prosaic that good one might be. I mean, it's worth reminding yourself that your hot water works or that you love music, isn't it? Try it. It does actually work.

LESSON 7:
CREATE A BEAUTIFUL WORKSPACE

Working from your shed or kitchen is fine, but wherever you work, make your space as beautiful as you can. Get comfortable chairs, a good set of speakers, some plants and a few well-chosen pictures. The more inspiring your workspace, the more productive you and your team will be. Aim to invest as much energy in decorating or styling your office as you do your home. An added benefit is that a great office attracts great staff at interview.

LESSON 8:
MEDITATE

Basic meditation isn't very difficult. Get an app, stick your headphones on and give it a go. It's great, and it works, especially in the morning.

Well, I suppose I'm pretty much done here.

In conclusion, teams are everything. They make life better, richer, more fun and more productive. Teams lift you up and carry you with them. Teams make good businesses great, and great organisations even better. Invest in your team and the world will be your oyster. From happy, engaged, motivated and empowered people comes magic.

Go, Team! Go!

And on that note, that's it from me.

I hope that you've found this useful, enjoyed it even. It's been a pleasure writing this for you and I am grateful to you for reading it. I never really think that anything I do is much good, and the more I read and reread and tweaked this, the more I wondered if it was doing something useful. But some kind friends (well, Caroline and my daughter, Tara) who have read it say it is, and I am happy to accept their wisdom. You know how it is: you can't see the wood for the trees sometimes and it takes a friend's perspective to straighten things out.

Whatever, I've poured my heart into it and offered up the lessons I've learned from a long time working alongside some incredible people. You could say it's a life's work. Thanks for putting your faith in me and joining me.

Don't forget to say 'hi' sometime. I hope we meet, but if we don't you can get in touch via my website *charliegladstone.com* or on Instagram, where I am called *@chasgladstone* and spend endless hours fiddling around and pressing that heart-shaped button. I'll get back to you, I promise.

Thank you very much.

Love from Chan x

ABOUT THE AUTHOR

Charlie Gladstone is an entrepreneur with 30 years'
experience operating small businesses. He is a retailer,
festival owner, farmer, author, publican, restaurateur,
podcast host, property developer, charity board member
and enthusiast. His businesses employ over 100 people
and include The Good Life Society, the Hawarden Estate
Farm Shop in North Wales and Glen Dye Cabins and
Cottages in Scotland. With his wife Caroline, he wrote
The Family Guide to the Great Outdoors (Penguin Random
House) and founded the homewares retailer Pedlars.
He has been married to Caroline for over 30 years and
together they have six adult children.

THANK

THANKS

Sincerest thanks to Miranda West for her faith, friendship and enthusiasm. Miranda, you are very clever.

Deep thanks to my fellow Do authors Mark Shayler, Anja Dunk and James Sills for their friendship and advice. And to Freddie Baveystock, David Bickerton and James Greenwood for always listening and responding with perfect advice. Thank you to Giles Andreae for being so encouraging as I sketched this out. And to Holly Tucker for inspiration and kindness.

Thanks to Matt Blease for his wonderful work over many years, and particularly here.

And while I'm at it — and I don't often get this sort of chance — thanks to all of my amazing friends for being amazing. I haven't told many of you I am writing this, but I know you'll buy lots of copies.

Thanks to my outstanding teams in London, Hawarden and at Glen Dye; truly, you are some of the best people I have been lucky enough to know and I am proud of what we achieve together. In particular, thanks to Alan Downes, Rachel Sedgwick and Anthony Hall, my seconds-in-command. But all of you are great.

Thanks to the whole team at the Do Lectures; you do what you do so very well.

Thanks to my dad for being the finest teacher anyone could hope for. Wherever you are, Dad, I'm sure you'd agree with some of this book and find other bits hilarious.

Most of all, as ever, thanks to Caroline, Jack, India, Tara, Xanthe, Kinvara, Felix, Reyhan, Dave and Aphra; we are the A team.

Books in the series

Also available

Available in print, digital and audio formats from booksellers or via our website: **thedobook.co**

To hear about events and forthcoming titles, you can find us on social media @dobookco, or subscribe to our newsletter